Samantha Roslund
and John Willis

Online Teamwork

DIGITAL CITIZENSHIP

LIGHTBOX
openlightbox.com

Go to **www.openlightbox.com** and enter this book's unique code.

ACCESS CODE

LBXP9655

Lightbox is an all-inclusive digital solution for the teaching and learning of curriculum topics in an original, groundbreaking way. Lightbox is based on National Curriculum Standards.

LIGHTBOX SUPPLEMENTARY RESOURCES

SHARE
Share titles within your Learning Management System (LMS) or Library Circulation System

CURRICULUM
Find national and state curriculum correlations

CITATION
Create bibliographical references following the Chicago Manual of Style

STANDARD FEATURES OF LIGHTBOX

AUDIO High-quality narration using text-to-speech system

ACTIVITIES Printable PDFs that can be emailed and graded

SLIDESHOWS Pictorial overviews of key concepts

VIDEOS Embedded high-definition video clips

WEBLINKS Curated links to external, child-safe resources

TRANSPARENCIES Step-by-step layering of maps, diagrams, charts, and timelines

INTERACTIVE MAPS Interactive maps and aerial satellite imagery

QUIZZES Ten multiple-choice questions that are automatically graded and emailed for teacher assessment

KEY WORDS Matching key concepts to their definitions

This title is part of our Lightbox digital subscription

Lightbox Grades 3–5 Subscription
ISBN 978-1-5105-5424-5

Access hundreds of Lightbox titles with our digital subscription. Sign up for a **FREE** subscription trial at **www.openlightbox.com/trial**

Online Teamwork

Contents

1 Chapter One

It Is All About Teamwork!

Try to imagine playing a game of tag by yourself. Think about how hard it would be to build a tree house without help. Working in groups makes many jobs easier. It also makes them much more fun! Each person has a different job to do when working in a group. There are many different ways people can work together. We are going to talk about working in teams online.

Many fun activities, such as tic-tac-toe, cannot be done without a friend to play with.

One great way to work with teammates online is to create a **wiki**. Wikis are web pages that many different people can edit. Taking care of a wiki is like taking care of a garden. A real garden needs hard work to grow, and so does your wiki. Once you and your team have decided on a topic or activity, you can follow these basic steps:

- **Plant**—create a wiki page and post thoughts about a topic
- **Dig**—**research** your wiki's topic to uncover more information
- **Water**—add pictures and new ideas to the wiki page
- **Weed**—correct mistakes on the wiki
- **Ponder**—step back and take time to think about what your team has learned

Wikipedia, one of the best-known wikis, has more than **6 million English articles**.

Across all languages, there are about **56 million** Wikipedia articles.

Much like a garden, a wiki will stop growing if left uncared-for.

The internet has many fun tools that make working together easy. However, remember to always stay safe online. Some sites may ask you for private information about yourself. Never share this information on the internet. Ask an adult if you are not sure about something. Safety is important.

When working with others on a project, it is useful to give and receive **feedback**. Everyone should have a chance to share ideas for improving your wiki. Feedback should always be positive and helpful. If you disagree with a teammate's idea, be polite and supportive. You should also be respectful when accepting feedback. Your teammates' ideas are just as important as your own!

Using polite words when giving feedback may make it easier for others to accept your advice.

People you work with online cannot see your face. They cannot hear your voice. This makes it hard for them to tell when you are just kidding. It is always a good idea to use polite words when working online.

Working as a team can lead to projects and ideas you might never have come up with on your own. Are you ready to start a wiki with your team?

Try This

Take a look at this list of information. Copy it onto a sheet of paper. Then put a checkmark in the "Private: Do Not Share" column or the "Okay to Share" column.

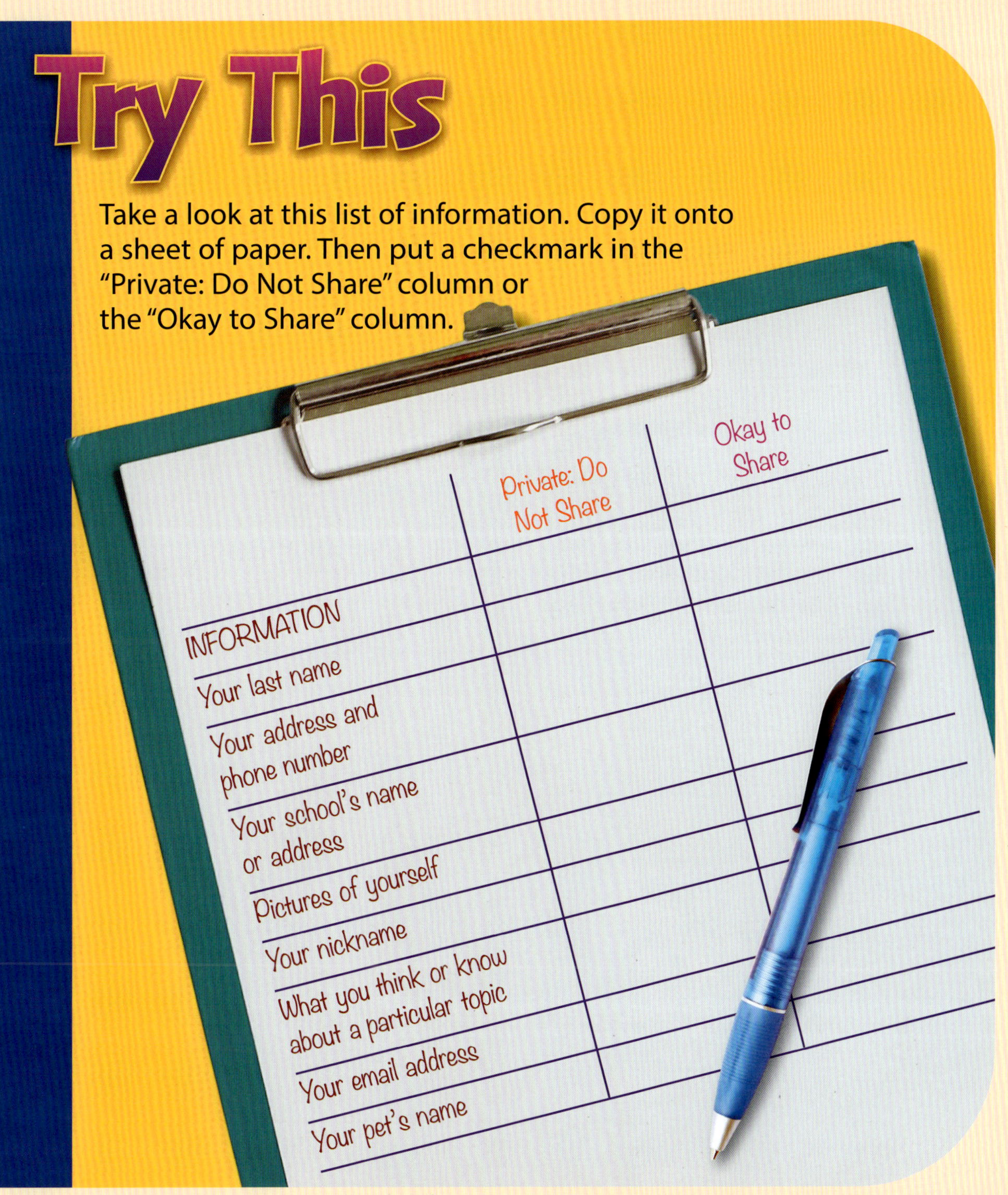

INFORMATION	Private: Do Not Share	Okay to Share
Your last name		
Your address and phone number		
Your school's name or address		
Pictures of yourself		
Your nickname		
What you think or know about a particular topic		
Your email address		
Your pet's name		

Did you mark the first four items on the list as private? These things should never be shared online. The last four items on the list are usually okay to share.

History of Wikis

1945

American engineer Vannevar Bush comes up with the idea for a series of interconnected articles.

1995

American programmer Ward Cunningham creates a website information organizing system called WikiWikiWeb.

2001

The online, user-edited encyclopedia Wikipedia is launched.

2006

English Wikipedia has more than 1 million articles.

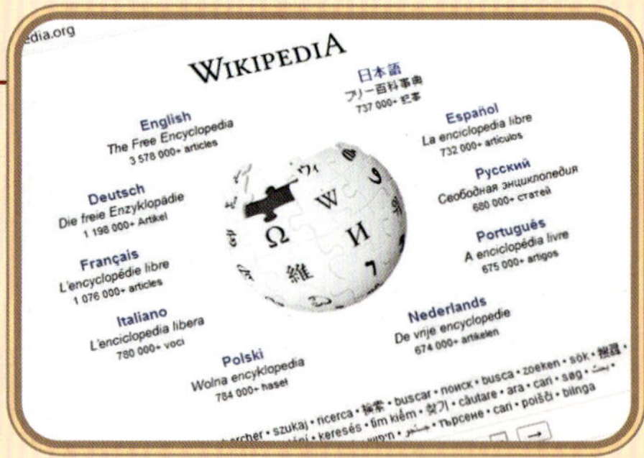

2011

More than 250 versions of Wikipedia exist in different languages.

2021

Wikipedia is one of the top 10 most-visited sites on the internet.

Mapping Wikis

St. Petersburg, Florida, 2003
The non-profit Wikimedia Foundation is formed in order to fund Wikipedia.

Oxford, United Kingdom, 2007
The Oxford English Dictionary officially adds the word *wiki*.

2 Chapter Two

Starting a Wiki

It is time to create a wiki! You will start your first wiki on your own. Your teammates will join in after it is created. Ask an adult to help you set up your wiki. Then, think of a topic for your wiki page. Do you love basketball? Chocolate ice cream? Frogs? Be creative with your ideas.

If writing a wiki about frogs, the information you add could include frog habitats, species, or conservation.

Useful information on a horse wiki could include how horseshoes are made.

Your next step can be watering your wiki. Imagine a wiki about horses. You might water it by adding facts about horseshoes. You could add a picture of a horse. Ask your teammates to do the same. Always give credit to ideas and pictures you find on other people's websites.

Now it is time to weed out mistakes. Check for spelling errors. Correct any facts that are wrong. Do not just delete someone else's work. If something is incorrect or does not belong, add it to the discussion page. You can usually find this section by clicking on a link at the top of the page.

After weeding, you can ponder. What was added to your wiki? How did this make it better? Ask these questions after each activity. Pondering pays off!

A good photo can make a wiki more fun to look at and easier to understand.

Try This

Follow these steps once you have an idea for your wiki:

1. Give your wiki page a title. Then, click the Edit button.
2. Add the headings "I Know" and "I Wonder."
3. Post three facts you know about your topic under "I Know."
4. Post three questions you are curious about under "I Wonder."
5. Ask an adult to help you invite your teammates to your new page.
6. Ask your teammates to visit the wiki. They can add what they know and wonder about your topic. Make sure everyone posts their ideas.

3 Chapter Three

Digging Deep

It is time for your team to choose another topic to explore. Begin by creating a new wiki. This time, work together with your group to select a topic. Remember that no idea is wrong or bad. Someone in your group might think of something completely new to you!

Use the discussion area on your wiki to post ideas for a new topic. Your team should discuss pros and cons for each possible topic. Then, each person can vote for his or her favorite one.

Creating a chart or table can make it easier to sort out pros and cons.

Finding multiple sources can help confirm any information found when researching a topic.

Once your team decides on a topic, list several "I Wonder" questions on the wiki page. Divide the questions up among the team members. You and your team will work on finding the answers to these questions. Each person should have an equal number of questions to research.

Now it is time to dig deep. Search for information in many different **sources**. Use websites and print sources to find interesting facts. Share any sources that might help your teammates with their research.

If you think something on your wiki should be changed, mention it on the discussion area.

Each team member should plant new information on the wiki. You can also check each other's work. Divide the wiki page into sections for each team member to weed. Is everything spelled correctly? Are the facts accurate? Does all of the information make sense?

Try This

It helps to look up information in more than one source. Choose one research question about your topic. If you are writing about iguanas, you might ask how big these lizards get. Have each group member look up the answer using a different source. Each team member should post his or her findings in your wiki's discussion section. Then, work together to answer these questions:

- What sources did we use?
- Did we all find the same information? What was the same? What was different?
- Did we find different answers? How do we know which one is right?

4 Chapter Four

Teaming Up for Fun

Your first two wikis helped you share information about certain topics. But wikis can also be used to organize other tasks.

Your group can team up online to plan a fun game day. Start by creating a new wiki page. Give it the title "Game Day." Use the wiki's discussion area to decide a time and a place. Make sure it is approved by everyone's parents or guardians. You should also discuss what kinds of games you will play. Will they be outdoor sports? Maybe you would rather play board games or video games. Each teammate should list a few suggestions. As a group, decide which games to play.

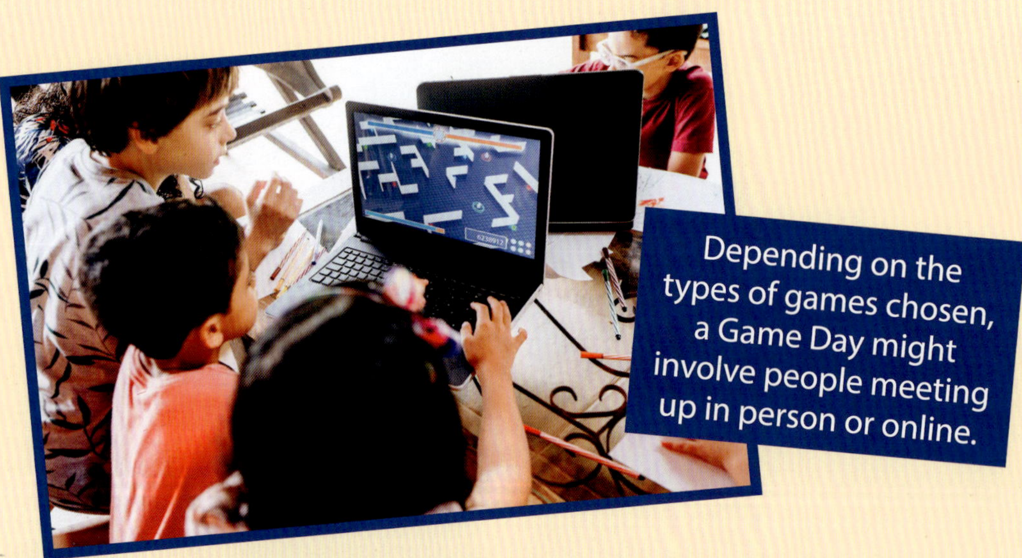

Depending on the types of games chosen, a Game Day might involve people meeting up in person or online.

Then, it is time to dig. Put one or two people in charge of each game. Have them organize what is needed for the game. Do they need any special equipment? What are the rules? Post this information on the Game Day wiki page. If anyone has ideas about each other's games, share them!

Try This

You have been working with your teammates online. You may need to team up offline for your Game Day, too. You can use your wiki to plan ahead. You and your teammates need to figure out each person's role in helping out with the Game Day. One person might host the event at his or her house. Another person might bring snacks. Someone else might bring sports equipment. Use the discussion area of your wiki to make a list of things you will need. Each group member can sign up to help out with a different task.

5 Chapter Five

Ponder Your Progress

Many gardeners enjoy sitting back and thinking about their hard work. They look at the beautiful plants in their garden. You should do the same with your wikis!

Remember to be SMART when teaming up online. Use this checklist to make sure you do not miss any tips.

SAFETY

- I did not share private information.
- I told an adult if I was asked to share private information.

MANNERS

- I used polite and respectful words in my posts.
- I posted my work in my own words.
- I offered positive feedback about my teammates' work.

ADULT SUPERVISION

- I asked an adult for permission before going online.

RESPONSIBILITY

- I realize that I am responsible for everything I have posted.
- I reported any **inappropriate** online content to an adult right away.

TEAMWORK

- I shared the lead and took turns.
- My work strengthened the work of my team.

Wikis change and grow like gardens do. Keep working with your teammates to plant, dig, water, weed, and ponder your wikis. What will your wikis look like as time goes on?

Try This

Think about how far your team and your wikis have come. Your team can use the discussion tab on your wikis to answer the following questions:

1. How has this wiki page changed since we first posted our topic?
2. What have we learned from these changes?
3. Should we invite more team members to help with this wiki? How could other people help improve our work?

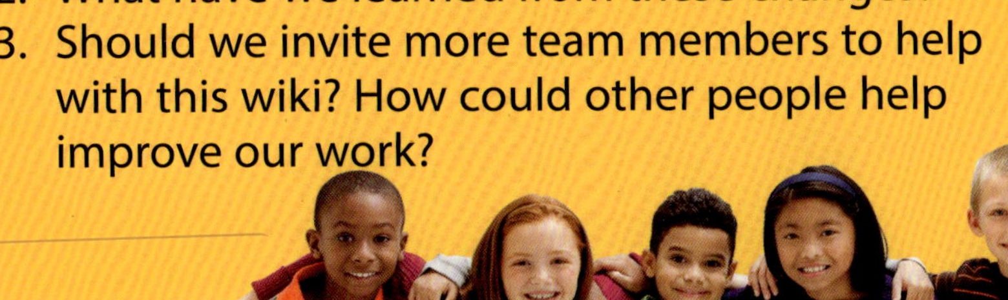

Quiz

1
How many versions of Wikipedia exist in different languages?

2
What helps confirm information you find when researching?

3
Where should you mention things on your wiki that you feel should be changed?

4
Who created WikiWikiWeb?

5
What are wikis?

6
Who should you tell if you are asked to share private information online?

7
Which American engineer came up with the idea for a series of interconnected articles?

8
What does it mean to "weed" a wiki?

9
What does SMART stand for?

10
What makes it hard for people online to tell if you are joking?

Answers: 1. More than 250 **2.** Finding multiple sources **3.** On the discussion area **4.** American programmer Ward Cunningham **5.** Web pages that many different people can edit **6.** An adult **7.** Vannevar Bush **8.** To correct mistakes **9.** Safety, Manners, Adult Supervision, Responsibility, Teamwork **10.** They cannot see your face

Key Words

feedback: reactions to something or comments about something

inappropriate: not right or proper for the situation, time, or place

research: collect information about a subject through reading, investigating, or experimenting

sources: documents, books, or websites that provide useful information

wiki: a website that allows users to change or add knowledge, information, or images

Index

LIGHTBOX

SUPPLEMENTARY RESOURCES

Click on the plus icon ⊕ found in the bottom left corner of each spread to open additional teacher resources.

- Download and print the book's quizzes and activities
- Access curriculum correlations
- Explore additional web applications that enhance the Lightbox experience

LIGHTBOX DIGITAL TITLES
Packed full of integrated media

VIDEOS

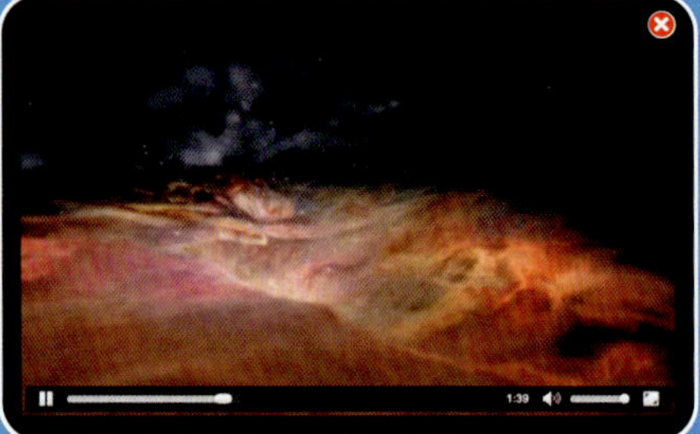

INTERACTIVE MAPS

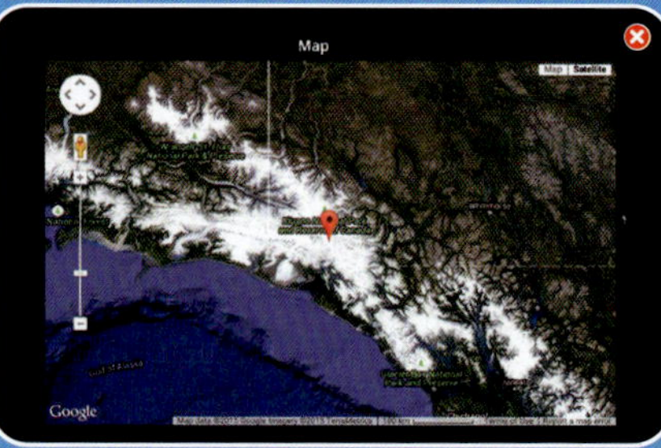

WEBLINKS

SLIDESHOWS

QUIZZES

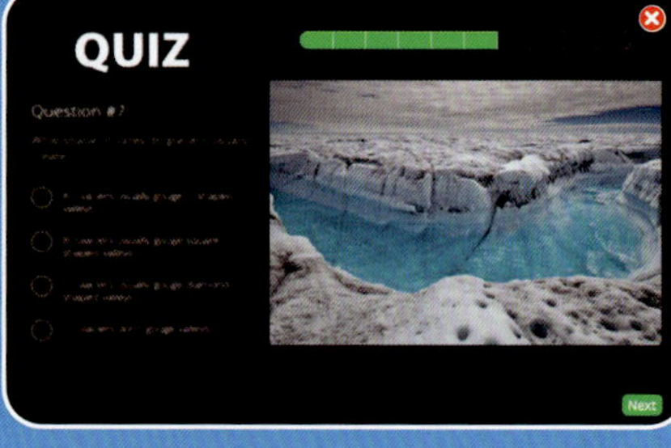

OPTIMIZED FOR
- ✓ TABLETS
- ✓ WHITEBOARDS
- ✓ COMPUTERS
- ✓ AND MUCH MORE!

Published by Lightbox Learning
276 5th Avenue
Suite 704 #917
New York, NY 10001
Website: www.openlightbox.com

First published by Cherry Lake Publishing in 2013

Library of Congress Control Number: 2021939449

ISBN 978-1-5105-5566-2 (hardcover)
ISBN 978-1-5105-5567-9 (multi-user eBook)

Printed in Guangzhou, China
1 2 3 4 5 6 7 8 9 0 25 24 23 22 21

082021
111020

Project Coordinator John Willis
Designer Jean Faye Marie Rodriguez

Photo Credits
Every reasonable effort has been made to trace ownership and to obtain permission to reprint copyright material. The publisher would be pleased to have any errors or omissions brought to its attention so that they may be corrected in subsequent printings.

The publisher acknowledges Alamy, Getty Images, and Shutterstock as its primary image suppliers for this title.